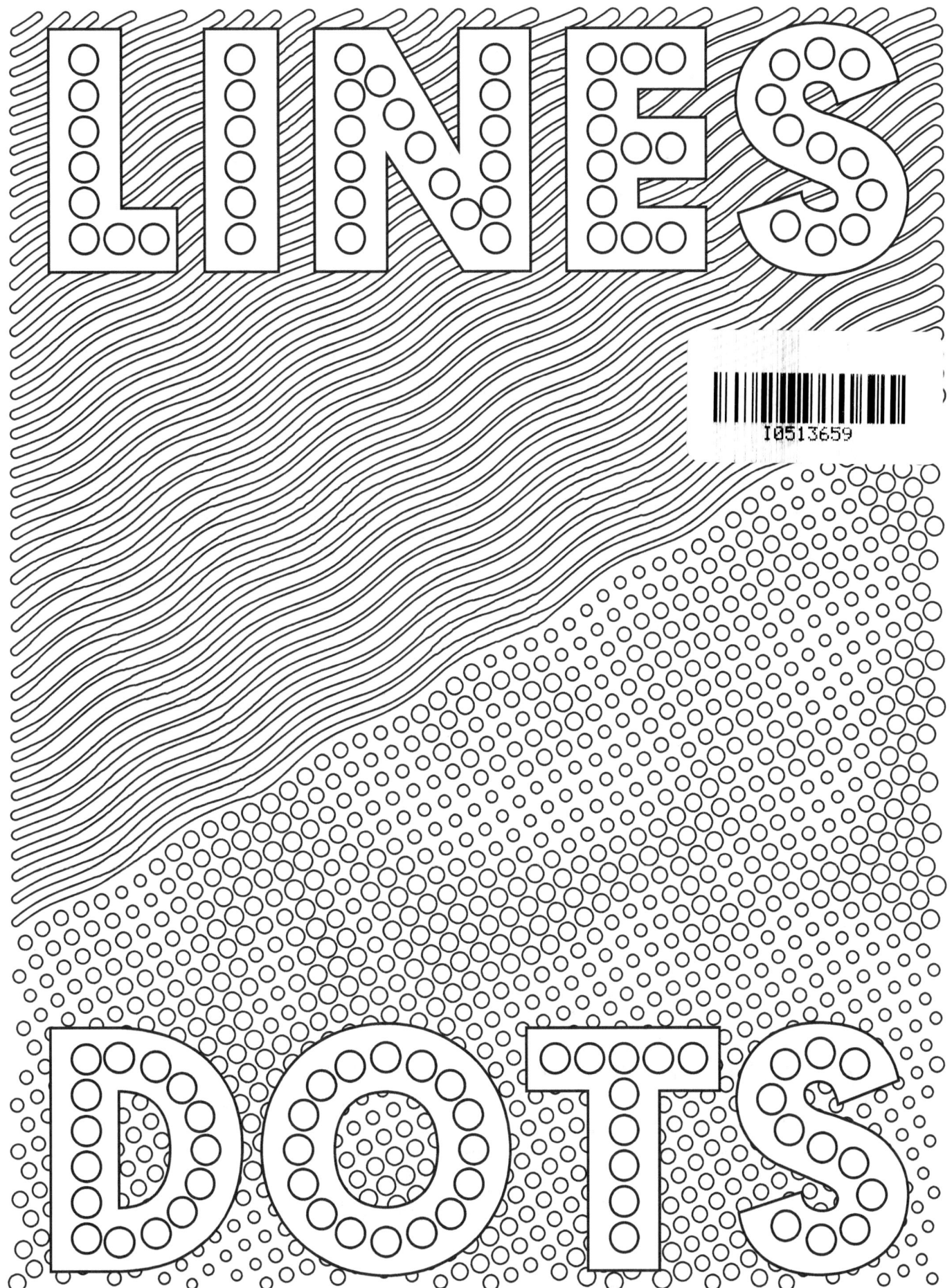

NO STRESS. NO THOUGHTS. NO EXTRA SKILLS. THIS PROCESS OF COLORING COULD BE COMPARED WITH WALKING AT A BIG DISTANCE WHEN YOUR BRAIN IS DISCONNECTED FROM VANITY AND IS PLUNGING INTO MEDITATION.

COLOR WITH ONE COLOR ANY OF 25 AMAZING PICTURES ON DIFFERENT TOPICS SUCH AS FAMOUS PEOPLE'S PORTRAITS, OBJECTS OF WORLD ART, SUBJECTS ABOUT NATURE ETC.

HALF IN LINES, HALF IN DOTS – CHOOSE THE QUEST ACCORDING TO YOUR MOOD. LISTEN TO THE RADIO, SOME MUSIC, SOME AUDIO-BOOK OR ENJOY YOUR INTERNAL HARMONY WHILE COLORING.

USING DARK SHADE COLORS OF PEN, PENCIL OR MARKER IS MORE PREFERABLE AS IT OPENS FANCY QUEST AND TRANSFORMS IT INTO A COMPLETE COMPOSITION.

LETTER-SIZE FORMAT AND LIGHTWEIGHT OF THIS UNIQUE LINES AND DOTS COLORING BOOK WILL ADD MORE FUN TO YOUR TRAVEL.

COPYRIGHT © 2018 BY SUNLIFE DRAWING
ALL RIGHTS RESERVED

NO PART OF THIS PUBLICATION MAY BE REPRODUCED, DISTRIBUTED, OR TRANSMITTED IN ANY FORM OR BY ANY MEANS, INCLUDING PHOTOCOPYING, RECORDING, OR OTHER ELECTRONIC OR MECHANICAL METHODS, WITHOUT THE PRIOR WRITTEN PERMISSION OF THE AUTHOR, EXCEPT IN THE CASE OF BRIEF QUOTATIONS EMBODIED IN CRITICAL REVIEWS AND CERTAIN OTHER NONCOMMERCIAL USES PERMITTED BY COPYRIGHT LAW.

MAIL@SUNLIFEDRAWING.COM
WWW.SUNLIFEDRAWING.COM

LINES

DOLPHIN
WATERMELONS
ALBERT EINSTEIN
CHESHIRE CAT
SWAN
MADONNA LITTA
LADYBUG
PURPLE CROCUS
BIRTHDAY CAKE
ELEPHANT
ROSE
DRAGON

DOTS

APHRODITE OF MELOS
IGUANA
SUNFLOWER
GAUTAMA BUDDHA
HONEY-BEE
HALLOWEEN PUMPKIN
PIKACHU
WHITNEY HOUSTON
ROOSTER
CHARLIE CHAPLIN
DONUTS

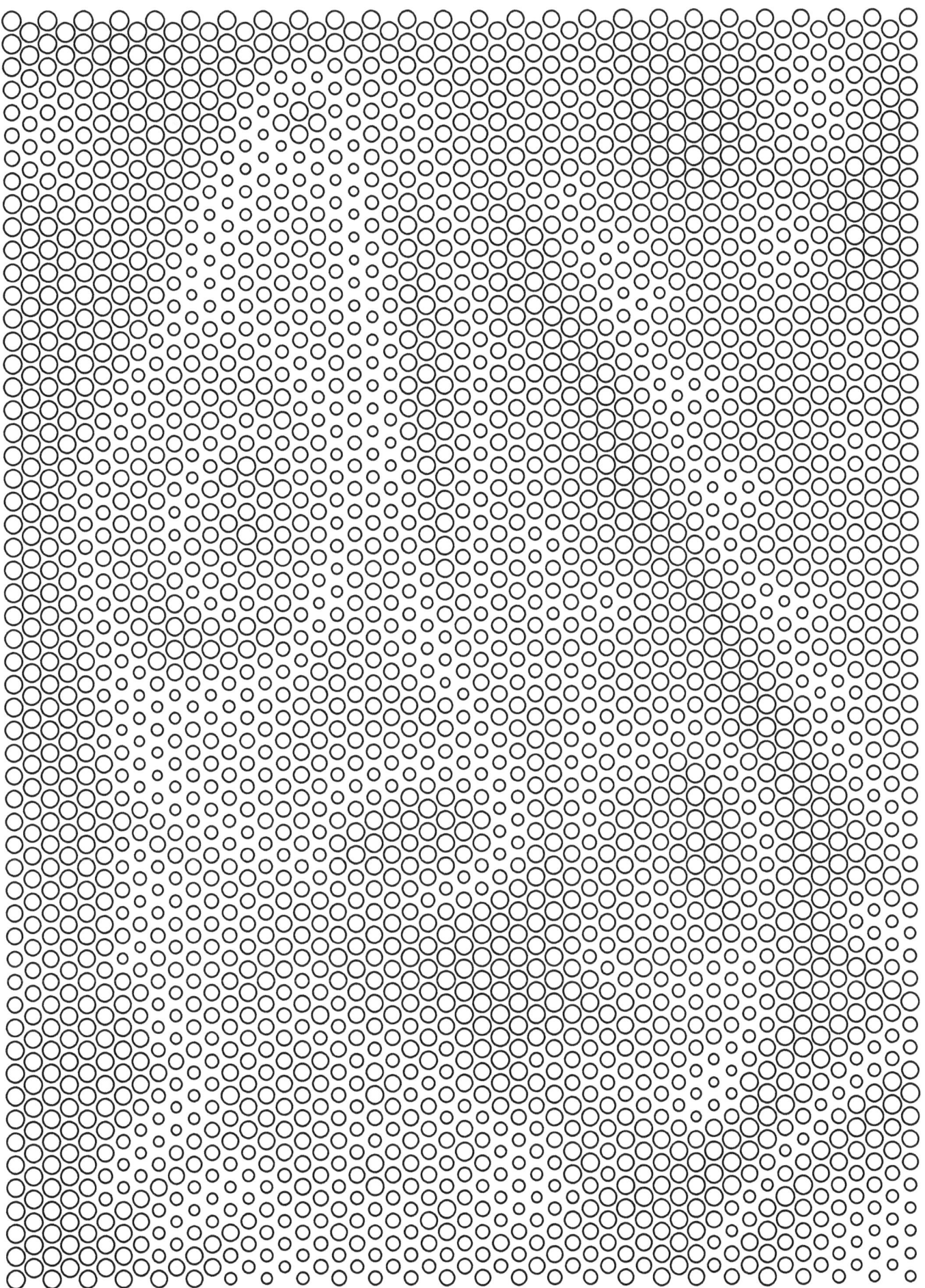

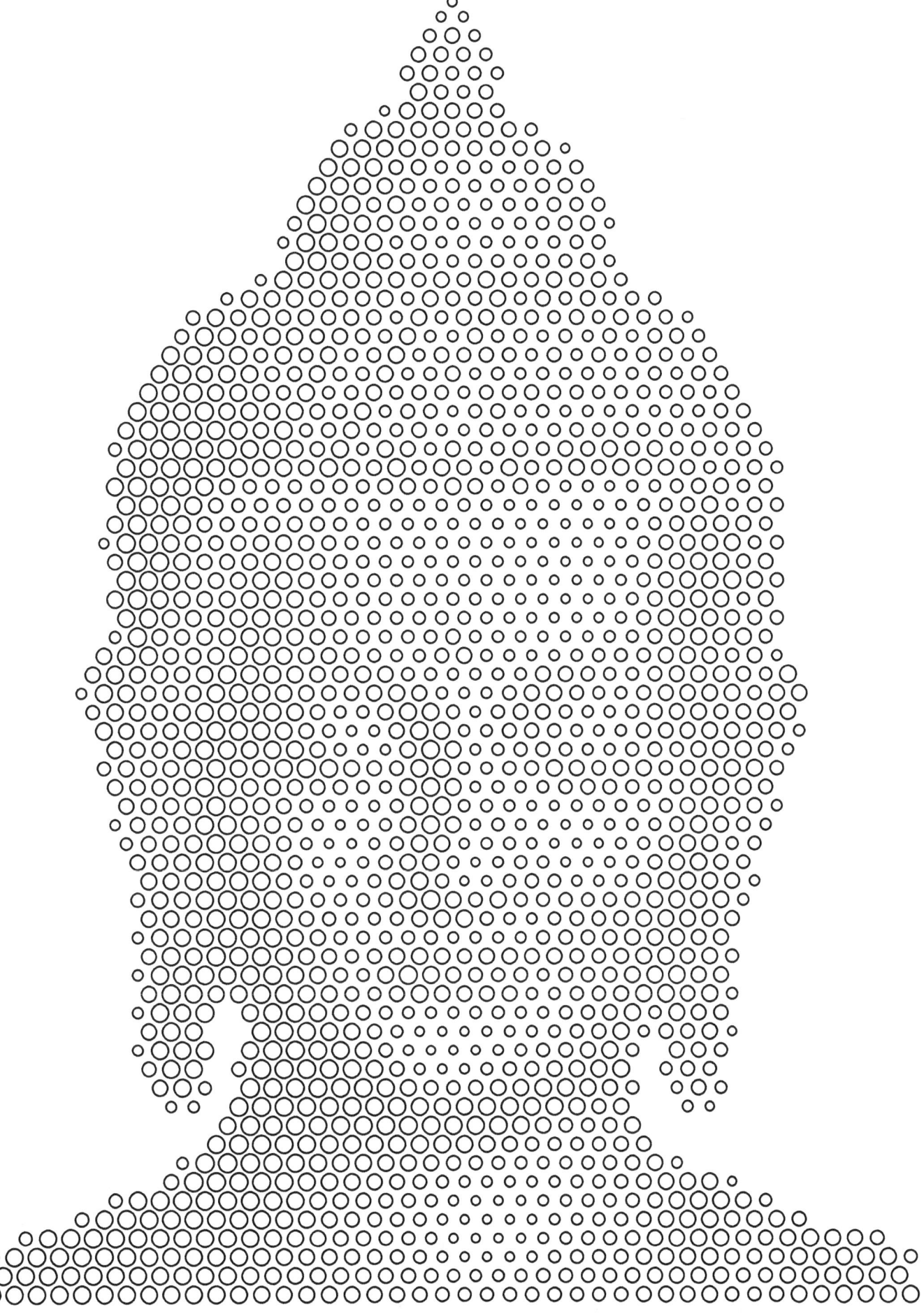

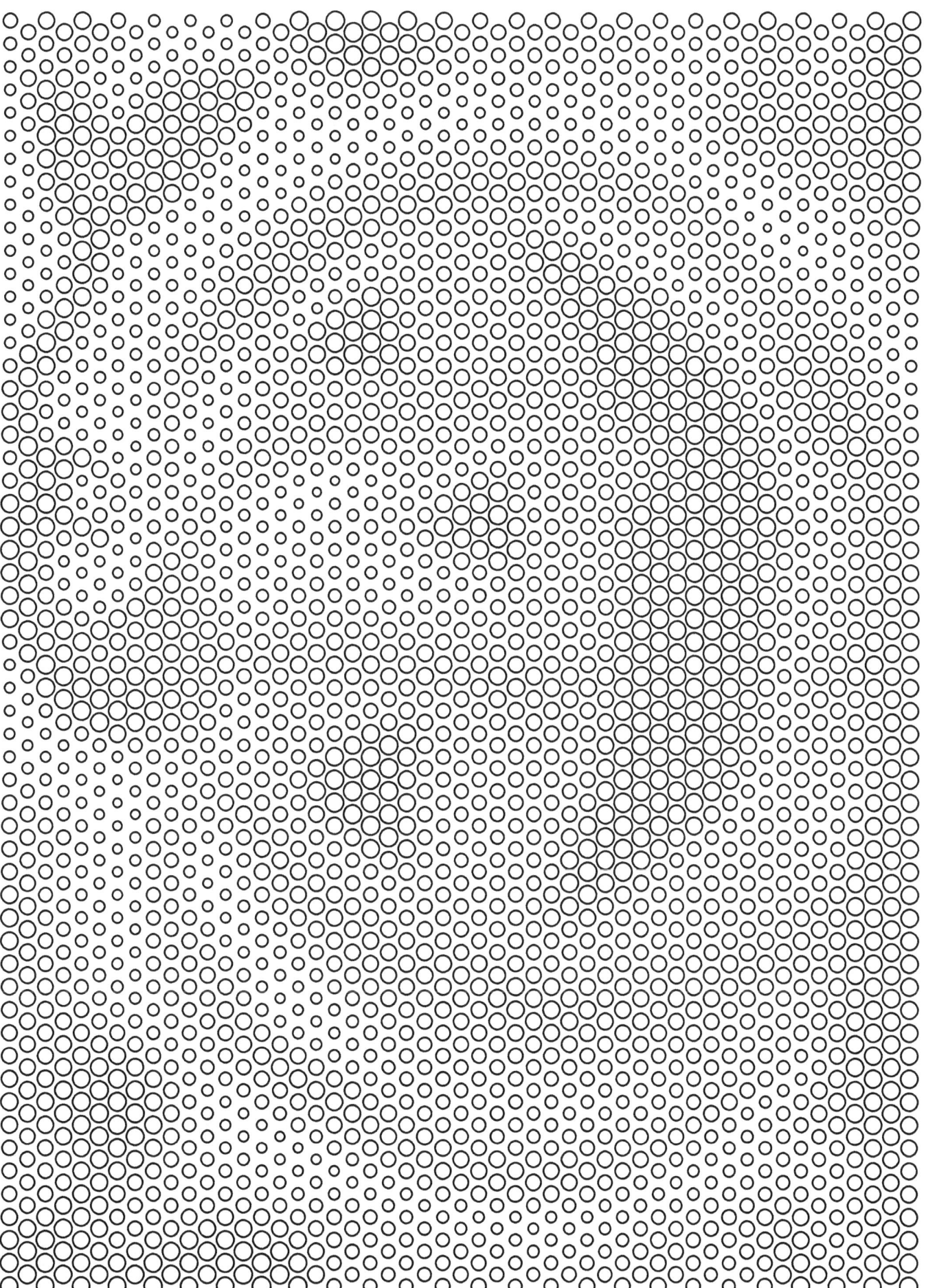

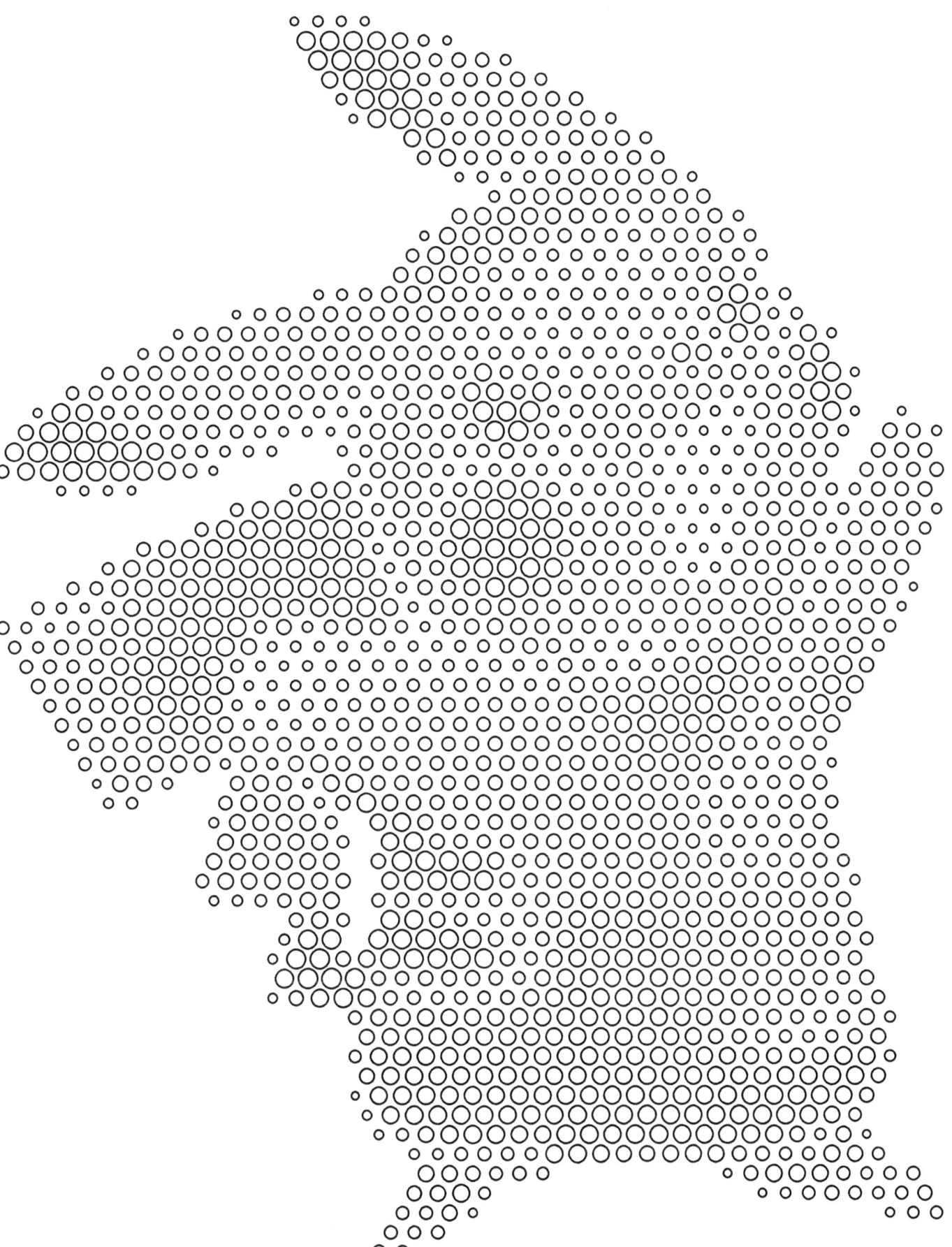

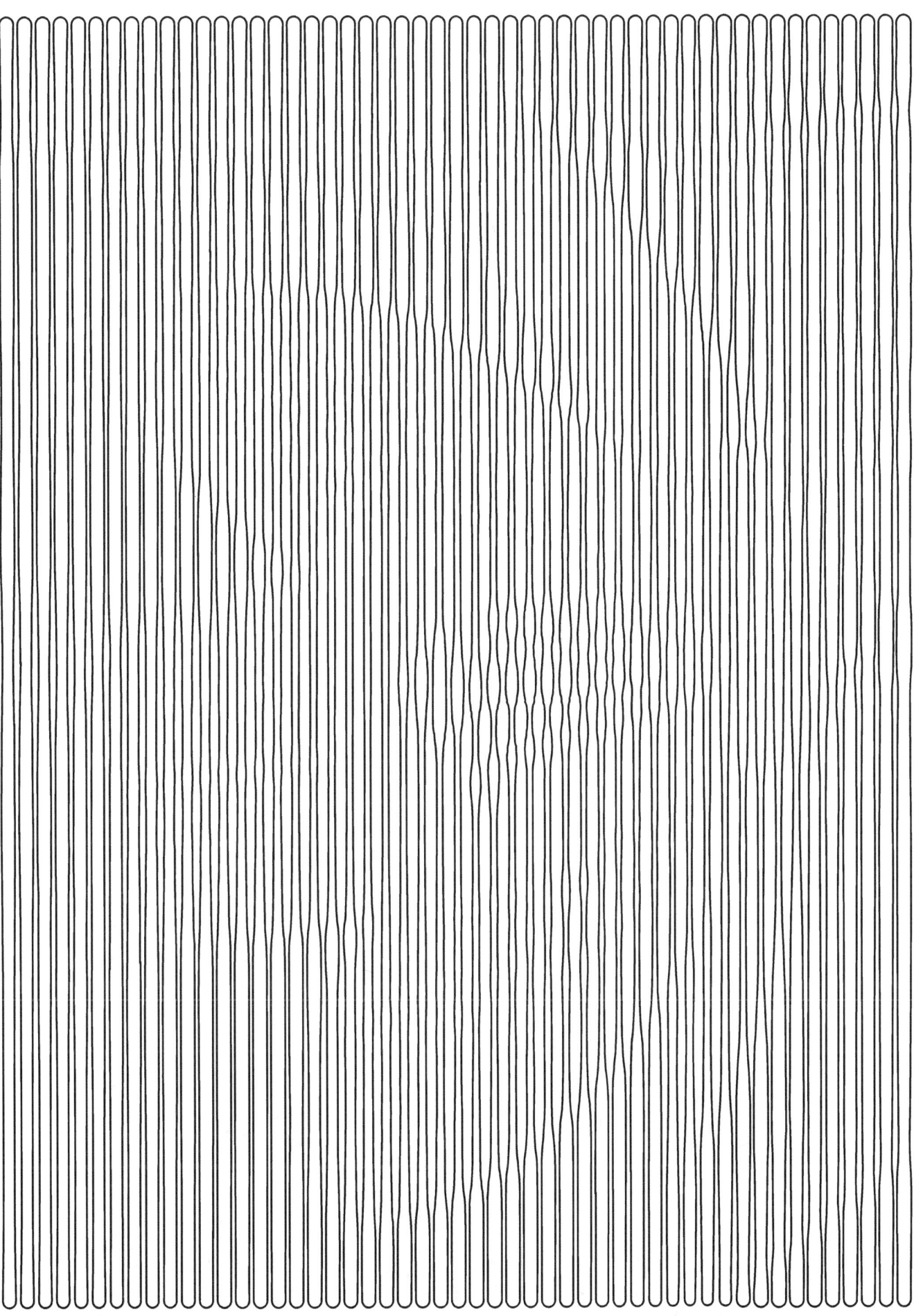

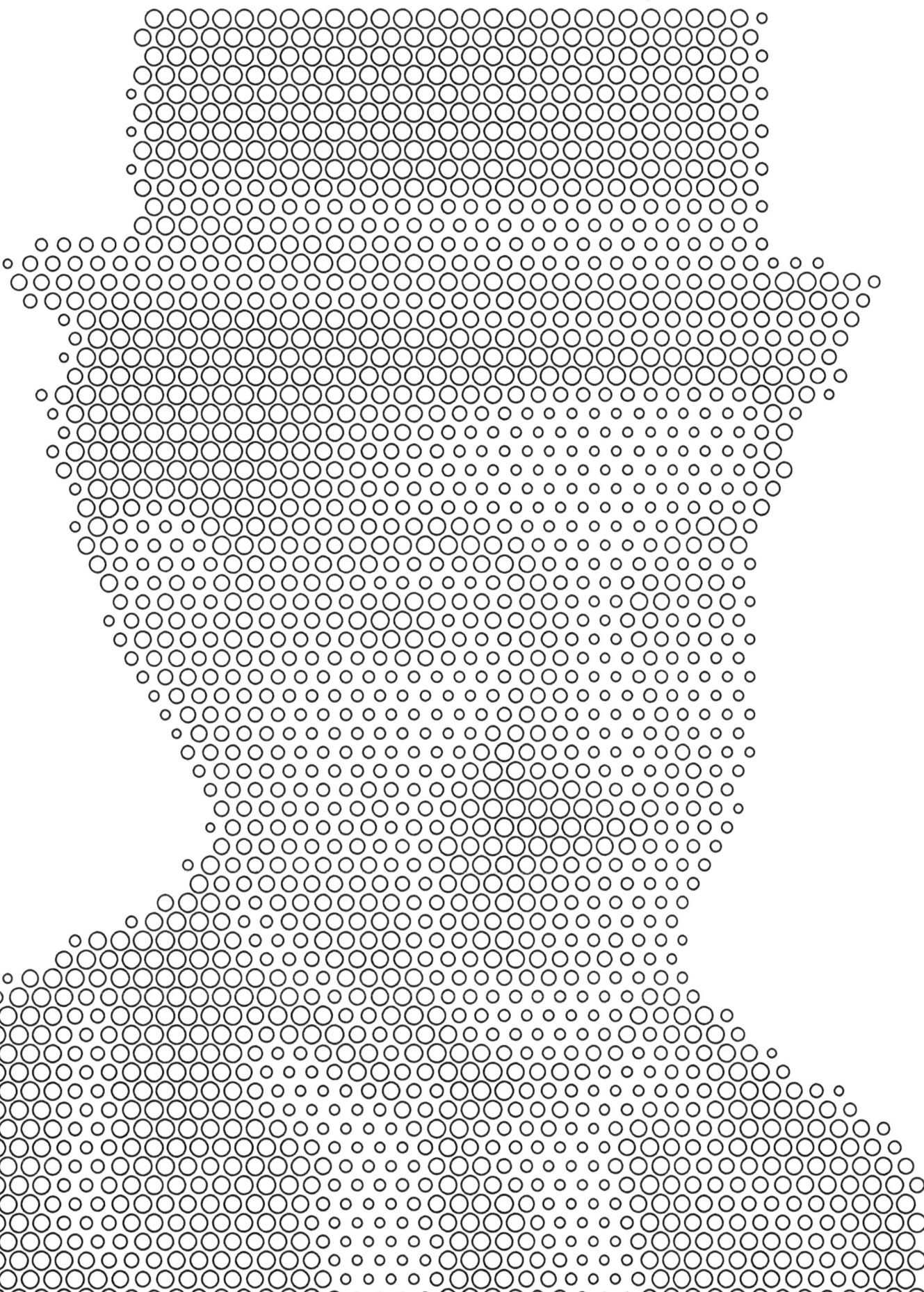

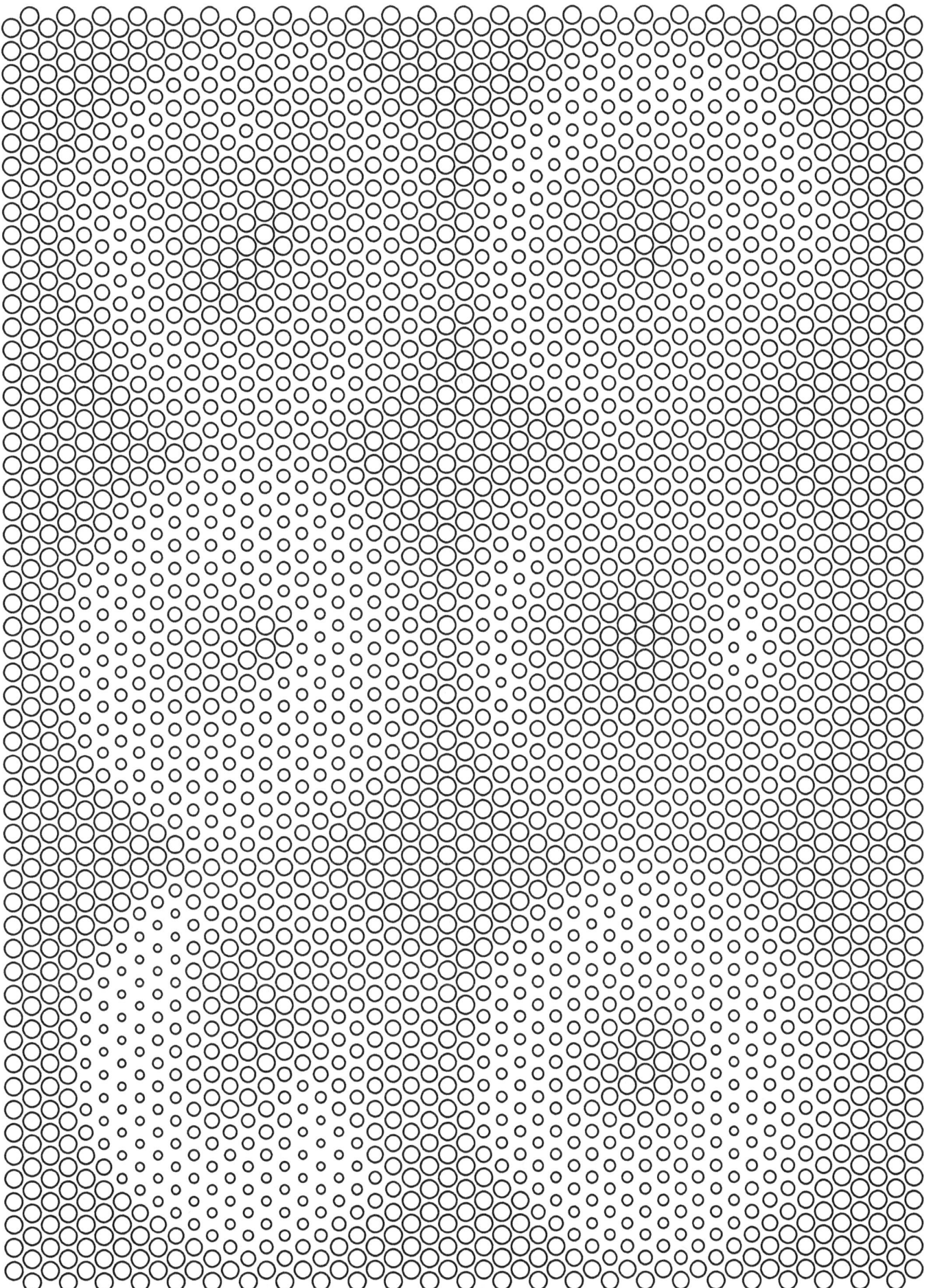

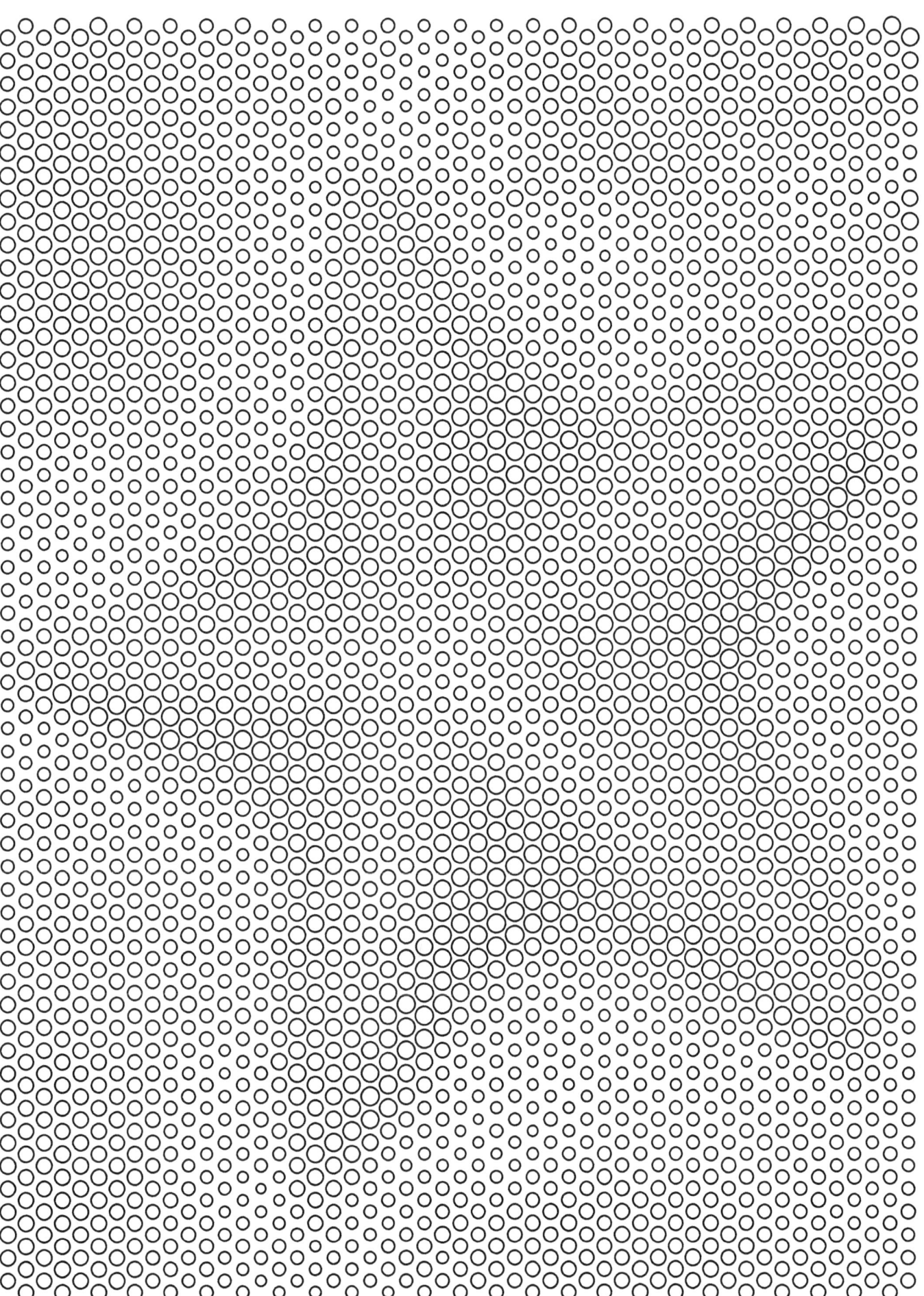

THANK YOU

FOR CHOOSING THIS BOOK! IF YOU ENJOYED IT, PLEASE WRITE YOUR REVIEW ON AMAZON. WE LOVE HEARING FROM OUR CUSTOMERS AND YOUR OPINION IS VERY IMPORTANT FOR US TO MAKE OUR BOOKS BETTER.

FOLLOW US

- FACEBOOK.COM/SUNLIFEDRAWING
- INSTAGRAM.COM/SUNLIFEDRAWING

www.ingramcontent.com/pod-product-compliance
Lightning Source LLC
Chambersburg PA
CBHW060005230526
45472CB00008B/1957